Martin —
w. warm greetings
as always,

Newman's London

affectionately

Joanna

May 2022

*For Father Christopher Pearson
of the Ordinariate of Our Lady of Walsingham.
With grateful thanks*

Newman's London

A pilgrim handbook

Joanna Bogle

Illustrated by Małgorzata Brykczyńska

GRACEWING

First published in England in 2019
by
Gracewing
2 Southern Avenue
Leominster
Herefordshire HR6 0QF
United Kingdom
www.gracewing.co.uk

The publishers have no responsibility for the persistence or
accuracy of URLs for websites referred to in this publication,
and do not guarantee that any content on such websites is, or
will remain, accurate or appropriate.

ISBN 978 085244 941 7

Typeset by Gracewing

Cover design by Bernardita Peña Hurtado

CONTENTS

Lead, kindly Light

Lead, kindly Light, amid th'encircling gloom,
lead Thou me on!
The night is dark, and I am far from home;
lead Thou me on!
Keep Thou my feet; I do not ask to see
The distant scene; one step enough for me.

I was not ever thus, nor prayed that Thou
shouldst lead me on;
I loved to choose and see my path;
but now lead Thou me on!
I loved the garish day, and, spite of fears,
Pride ruled my will. Remember not past years!

So long Thy power hath blest me, sure it still
will lead me on.
O'er moor and fen, o'er crag and torrent,
till the night is gone,
and with the morn those angel faces smile,
which I have loved long since, and lost awhile!

Meantime, along the narrow rugged path,
Thyself hast trod,
Lead, Saviour, lead me home in childlike faith,
Home to my God.
To rest forever after earthly strife
In the calm light of everlasting life.

JOHN HENRY NEWMAN

FOREWORD

GOING ON PILGRIMAGE to a great shrine, whether it is Lourdes or Santiago de Compostella or our own Walsingham here in England, is a central part of our Christian tradition. A pilgrimage reminds us that our lives, as individuals and families, and as a community in the Church here on earth, are a journey to God and guided by God. On pilgrimage, as in life, we seek out God's will, trusting in Jesus as our Way, Truth and Life.

Tracing the life of a saint is also a way of doing this. God raises up saints in all times and places, giving us examples to follow and stories to inspire and challenge us.

John Henry Newman, declared Blessed in a Mass celebrated by Pope Benedict XVI in Birmingham during his 2010 visit to Britain, was a man of the modern era who can make the idea of sainthood accessible to us. His Britain was a place of railways and large growing cities, of increasingly rapid travel and communication, and great debates about the future. His insights continue to inspire us in the twenty-first century with its even greater changes.

This book guides us through Newman's London. It is intriguing to discover the places that he knew. The house where he was born, near his father's bank in the City, no longer stands but the Square Mile is still a teeming place of banking and business. The rural Ealing, where he arrived in a stagecoach for boarding-school, has vanished under suburban streets. The family's summer home along by the Thames at Ham, however, still has an air of peaceful country living.

For Londoners and visitors alike, discovering Newman's London can bring the story of this great man's life into focus. It is a wonderful way of exploring the message that he has for us today.

I wish all pilgrim readers of this book every blessing and joy!

✠ Cardinal Vincent Nichols

Archbishop of Westminster

INTRODUCTION

T HE STRONG AND continuing interest in John Henry Newman, particularly now with his canonisation, brought the thought that pilgrims might find it useful to have a guide to places in London associated with him: where he was born, where he grew up, where he spent childhood summers ... the places of which he had warm memories, later recalled during his long life.

The cities with which Newman is chiefly associated are of course Oxford and Birmingham, so this book obviously has information on these. Guidebooks to both cities give due attention to this great figure. But the visitor to London who seeks information about Newman has hitherto not been given much help. This book is an attempt to remedy that.

The book is designed not only to help the Newman pilgrim on travels, but also to be read simply for enjoyment, and to provide background information on Newman's life and the importance he has in our country's Christian story.

Newman's London would not have been possible without the practical help of Jackie Brooks, who accompanied the author on various exploratory journeys around London, always with good humour and a sense of fun. Warm thanks, too, to Amanda Hill for pilgrim journeys, books, information, and enthusiastic support, and to the Sisters of The Work at Littlemore for a wonderful welcome and much help. A special gratitude is owed to Małgorzata Brykczyńska for her lovely illustrations. Somehow all of this echoed Newman's own message on the value of true friendship. Newman scholars helped the author to understand and value the greatness of Newman's contribution to the Church, notably Father James Tolhurst, and Dr and Mrs A. J. Nash. To them, for this and for much more, the author expresses affectionate thanks.

NEWMAN'S LIFE AND MESSAGE

JOHN HENRY NEWMAN is the most significant figure in English Christianity in modern times. Born in 1801, and dying in 1890, Newman's life effectively spanned the nineteenth century. His childhood memories included celebrations for the victory of the Battle of Trafalgar in the age of sail—as an old man he lived in a city of trams and factories, with suburbs beginning to spread over what was once farmland.

Newman studied at Oxford and was ordained in the Church of England. He became the leader of the major revival and realignment in the Church of England in the middle of the nineteenth century, which gave it a whole new sense of purpose and direction. Through Newman and his fellow Tractarians, the Church of England looked back beyond the Reformation to the previous centuries of Christianity and began a debate about its own history and mission which was to have far-reaching consequences.

As Newman made his own progress beyond that, into the Catholic Church, he began a new journey which was to accomplish more than anyone at that time could have imagined. He was received into the Catholic Church in 1845 by Blessed Dominic Barberi, a Passionist missionary priest. It seemed to many people a strange and even obscure thing to do—and

over the next years it would involve Newman in much
distress and many difficulties. At the behest of others
he undertook immensely challenging tasks—such as
the planned Catholic University in Ireland—that
proved frustrating and seemed to achieve little. His
courage in standing up for the Catholic faith brought
him a libel action with a long drawn out legal case that
could have seen him sent to prison. He was misunderstood in Rome and within his own family.

But his books and sermons, widely read for the next
century and into the twenty-first, have had far-reaching consequences. He helped to build up a revived
Catholicism which with its ideas and its language, its
sense of history and its understanding of being in
unity with the Church of all time, ushered in a new
way of thinking about religion in Britain. By the time
he died, he was a revered figure, and the full effect of
his contribution would unfold over time and today is
more strongly felt than ever.

John Henry Newman's understanding of religious
freedom, of the supreme demands of pursuing truth,
and of a Church unshackled from the State, helped to
shape the message that Pope Benedict brought to
Britain at the start of the twenty-first century. When
Pope Benedict XVI arrived in Britain to beatify John
Henry Newman in 2010, there was no lack of
comment and debate. But the old-style comfortable
anti-Catholicism of a kind assumed to be normal from
the 17th century to the early 20th, had vanished.
Anyone attempting to revive old "No Popery" slogans
would have seemed odd and unconvincing. Opposi-
tion to the Pope came from campaigners whose highly

vocal objections concerned aspects of Christian moral teaching. They were angry that Christians would dare to challenge fashionable ideology on sexual matters. But the general public response to the Papal visit was one of interest, respect and even enthusiasm with an atmosphere of unity and goodwill.

Newman has been called the "father of the Second Vatican Council", the major gathering of the world's bishops in the middle of the twentieth century. Following two world wars involving millions of victims, the Council sought to find ways to evangelise anew, to offer the truth to the human race which had involved itself in bloodshed and horror on an unprecedented scale. Both wars had begun in Europe, heartland of Christianity over the centuries, where the majority of people were baptised, and most laws and customs were framed reflecting Christianity. There was a recognition that something must have gone wrong: nations that were officially Christian had twice lined up to slaughter each other.

Newman's influence could be seen in the Council's study of the early Church Fathers, in its emphasis on truth, and its understanding of the Church's mission as being rooted in truth rather than in the establishment of formal bonds of Church and State.

Newman's vision was often misunderstood in his lifetime, and has been misunderstood and misinterpreted since. He was firmly, and passionately, against liberalism in religion and rejected outright the notion that truth could or should be adapted to meet fashionable demands. God's plan for men and women is centred on the fact that he came to live among us: the truth of the Christian faith is non-negotiable.

Those who have found inspiration in Newman have included St Edith Stein, the Jewish philosopher who became a Carmelite nun and perished in Auschwitz, and the "White Rose" anti-Nazi young German students who were executed in Munich for distributing leaflets denouncing Nazi ideology and crimes.

Suffering—as Newman found and understood– is an inescapable part of an authentic following of Christ, and the Christian life of prayer is bound up with sacrifice. We are not here just to be comfortable: there is joy and beauty and goodness in life and God wants us to know him through these things, but the encounter will also involve being challenged and having to make decisions to do what is right and to trust in God's plans and providence.

DISCOVERING NEWMAN'S LONDON

THIS BOOK HAS been produced for pilgrims who have come to love John Henry Newman and want to know more about him.

Newman was a Londoner, born in the heart of the City, near the Bank of England. His long life took him to places that have since become strongly associated with him, most importantly Oxford and Birmingham, but also Dublin and of course Rome. But London can rightly claim him as a native son, and the pilgrim who seeks to walk in his footsteps will find London an excellent place in which to start.

The London that Newman knew became, during his lifetime, the centre of a great worldwide empire. In the nineteenth century Britain was the greatest power on earth: laws passed in London bound people in Africa and Asia and Australasia; decisions made in London drew boundaries on maps, forged treaties and alliances, fostered trade, began and concluded wars.

Today's London is unimaginably different. Two world wars, the loss of empire, and massive immigration with a consequent mix of races and religions, languages and cultures, have made the London—and the Britain—of the nineteenth century something that is utterly remote from that of the 21st. This makes it the more extraordinary that John Henry Newman's words speak to us today with a message that is as

relevant and as forceful, as challenging and as poign-
ant as when he wrote them—indeed in some cases
more so, as his life and writings were in many ways
prophetic.

We will encounter Newman chiefly in his message,
his example of prayer and holiness, his courage and
faithfulness in difficulties, his theological insight and
his passion for truth and for clarity in presenting it.
But perhaps we can also find glimpses of him as we
visit the places where he lived and studied and worked
and prayed. We can visit these places, fascinated by
his story and conscious that, like pilgrims down all
the centuries, we can invoke his intercession in prayer
and ask his assistance on our own spiritual journeying.

NEWMAN'S BIRTHPLACE

O N AN OFFICE block, in a street at the back of the Bank of England, a square blue marbled stone announces: "In a house near this spot John Henry Cardinal Newman was born 21st February 1801". The house in which Newman was born no longer stands. The blue plaque is at 60, Threadneedle Street, London EC2R 8HP. The Newman family home was actually numbered as 80, Old Broad Street.

Newman's father was a banker, and the family was living at the centre of the banking world, in the Square Mile of the City of London.

The blue square commemorative stone—it is one of the City's own special commemorative stones, not a circular blue plaque from English Heritage—is set in the wall where the massive block of 60, Threadneedle Street slightly recedes from the street and a large modern sculpture called "City Wing" by Christopher le Brun stands in a paved area. 60 Threadneedle Street houses a number of banks and investment companies. The next building along is number 125 Old Broad Street.

60 Threadneedle Street is also the address of a Brasserie Blanc Restaurant—where the author of this guide obtained refreshment on a hot day and was made most welcome—and the blue plaque is on the buttress that divides the office block from the restaurant.

Newman's parents were John and Jemima (née Fourdrinier) Newman. They married in 1799 at St Mary's church at Lambeth. John Newman's bank was Ramsbottom, Newman and Company in Lombard Street, and the family home was nearby. There were six children of whom John Henry was the oldest. His two brothers were Charles (b. 16 June 1802) and Francis (b. 27 June 1805); his sisters were Harriet (b.10 December 1803), Jemima (b.19 May 1808) and Mary (b. 9 November 1809). His mother (1772–1836) came from a well-known Huguenot Protestant family who settled in Britain after being hounded out of France because of their religious beliefs. An ancestor was Paul Fourdrinier, an engraver, printer and stationer, who became well known.

Jemima's father was Henry Fourdrinier, who died in 1799, some eighteen months before Newman was born. Her brothers were Henry (1766–1854) Charles (1767–1841) John Rawson (1770–1836) and Sealy (1774–1847), and her sister was Mary (dates uncertain).

John Henry Newman was baptised on April 2nd, 1801 at the church of St Benet Fink which then stood in Threadneedle Street. His godfather was Richard Ramsbottom who with his nephew John was a partner in John Newman's bank. Both Ramsbottoms in turn became Members of Parliament.

The church of St Benet Fink or Finch was established in the 13th century: it was burned down in the Great Fire of London in 1666, and a new one—in which Newman would be baptised—was built, designed by the famous Sir Christopher Wren. This building was pull down in the 1840s—halfway through Newman's life—as part of a reworking of the road system in this part of the City, following a fire that burned down the Royal Exchange. Another church, St Bartholomew-by-the-Exchange was pulled down at the same time. St Benet's was pulled down in two stages—first just the tower was removed, in 1842, and a new church entrance made so that the building could still be used for worship. But this proved unsatisfactory and so in 1848 the whole building came down.

There were protests over the demolition of St Benet's, but it went ahead because there were—and still are—a great many churches within the City, several within easy walking distance of Threadneedle Street. The parish was combined with a neighbouring one, St Peter le Poer.

"Benet" is another way of saying "Benedict" and the church was dedicated to the famous St Benedict, founder of Western monasticism, who gave his name to the Benedictine Order of monks and nuns. The "Fink" part is the name of Robert Fink (or Finch) who paid for the church in the 13th century. There was probably an earlier Saxon church on the same site.

The proceeds from the sale of St Benet's were used to build a new church of the same name in what was the then semi-rural suburban district of Tottenham.[1]

John Henry Newman's birth in the City makes him a true Londoner: he was born just yards from the Thames, a few minutes' walk from St Paul's Cathedral, not far from the Tower, and within the sound, on a clear day, of the Bow bells.

How to get to Newman's birthplace

Nearest tube station: BANK. You can approach Threadneedle Street by walking northwards from Bank station. The tube station has several exits: Threadneedle Street and the Bank of England are labelled. If you find you are walking along Poultry, or along Queen Victoria Street, you are going in the wrong direction.

The Bank of England is a major London landmark and Threadneedle Street runs alongside and behind it. It is easily reached on foot from other major landmarks such as St Paul's Cathedral and the Tower of London. It is not recommended to take a car into the City of London and there are no parking places near the Bank of England.

NUMBER 17 SOUTHAMPTON PLACE, LONDON WC1 2AJ

WHEN NEWMAN WAS two years old, the family moved to a large London house at 17 Southampton Street—the name of the road has now been changed to Southampton Place—near Bloomsbury Square, where his father's bank had its headquarters. This was to be their London home for the next years and a large plaque now commemorates this: "Here lived, in early life, John Henry Cardinal Newman. Born 1801 died 1890." The family lived here from 1803 until 1816. For part of that time, they also had a large country house at Ham, near Richmond—of which more shortly.

Newman's younger brothers and sisters were born at 17 Southampton Place. Charles (b. 16 June 1802) would cause the rest of the family much worry over the years as he tried various careers, ran into debt and became something of a recluse. Francis (b. 27th June 1805) would become a distinguished classical scholar, author of several books, and professor of Latin at University College, London, near his birthplace. Like his brother John Henry, he developed a great interest in theology, but took a different path, becoming an extreme Evangelical and at one point joining the Plymouth Brethren. Towards the end of his life he abandoned traditional Christian beliefs becoming Unitarian, and he energetically supported various causes ranging from vegetarianism to women's suffrage. He is commemorated on the Reformers' Memorial in Kensal Green cemetery. Harriet (b. 10 Dec 1803) married Rev. Thomas Mozley (1806–1893), a prominent member of the Tractarians and author of several books. He was for many years a leader-writer on *The Times* newspaper. Harriet wrote hymns and popular books for children. Jemima (b.1808) married John Mozley (1808–1879), brother of Thomas: she was a prolific correspondent with Newman and their letters to one another have provided much material for Newman's biographers. Mary (b.1809) was Newman's favourite sister, much missed when she died young in 1828.

The house at 17 Southampton Place is now the London home of an American university, the Arcadia University, and is part of its Global Studies programme. It is possible to knock and ask for entrance: when this author did so, a courteous lady at the reception desk allowed us a brief view of the hall and an adjoining room. Naturally nothing remains that is linked with Newman, but the general layout appears to be the same as when the family occupied it, with large rooms leading off from the hall and a staircase leading up to what would have been bedrooms and the nursery.

The rather grand plaque on the outside wall was evidently placed there by a former owner as a piece of private initiative: it is not the standard circular blue plaque.

Today, this is very much university territory: the district is associated with University College, London. The land was at one time owned by the Earl of Southampton, hence the name of the street. The University College website notes that Southampton Place is "not to be confused with Southampton Place off Euston Road, nor with the Southampton Street leading from Covent Gardens to the Strand, or the Southampton Street (formerly Hampstead Street and now Conway Street) leading to Fitzroy Square."[2]

This area was developed in the 17th century for well-to-do families—close enough to the City for convenience, but far enough away to allow for large, comfortable airy houses to be built. Among famous people associated with Southampton Place are Colley Cibber, the 18th century actor and poet who lived here as a child, and in the early nineteenth century the theologian Isaac Williams, whose father was a barrister.

While living at 17 Southampton Place, the Newman family worshipped at St George's Church, Bloomsbury, and it was here that Newman's brothers and sisters were baptised: records note that Francis was baptised on 27th June 1805. The church—consecrated in 1730—had been built specifically to serve the families of this attractive area and had been expanded in 1781.

The Arcadia University seems proud of being in the London University district, and the literary associations of the area, but does not seem particularly interested in Newman. In their literature for American students they announce:

> We are located in the heart of the renowned literary area of Bloomsbury, London's university quarter, which is bustling with activity in the arts, education and medicine and is a short walk from Covent Garden, the West End theatre district and a multitude of shops, restaurants and entertainment venues.[3]

The Newman family left Southampton Place in 1816, when John Newman's bank closed. The Battle of Waterloo had ended the Napoleonic wars, but the victory was followed by hard economic times. Newman's father was able to pay the bank's creditors, but had to use all his own money in the process. The family had to leave their London home. They went initially to the family cottage at Norwood where they had earlier spent holidays, and then moved to Alton in Hampshire where John Newman tried, unsuccessfully, to start a brewery with the Ramsbottoms, his former banking partners. Meanwhile, young John Henry was at school in Ealing.

How to get to 17 Southampton Place

Nearest tube station is HOLBORN. Walk down Kingsway, heading north, then turn right into High Holborn, then into Southampton Place. The walk will take you about two minutes.

GREY COURT HOUSE, HAM, NEAR RICHMOND

THE VILLAGE OF Ham is on the south bank of the Thames, between the towns of Richmond and Kingston. The name comes from the Saxon *heim*, meaning home, and is common across England: Cheltenham, Twickenham, Birmingham, Chippenham, Walsingham ... and Tower Hamlets, the small villages clustered near the Tower of London.

The Newman family's country house, Grey Court House, at Ham, was described in his later years by John Henry Newman as his "house of dreams". He had golden, happy memories of the years there—his earliest years, because the family left Grey Court House when he was just six years old. The family lived there for just three years, from 1804 to 1807.

It was at Grey Court House that Newman lay in bed as a small boy and watched candles being placed in the windows to mark the victory of Trafalgar in 1805, something that he would remember all his life.

The house is a large, fine building facing on to Ham Street, leading down to the river. In Newman's day there would have been few other houses in the vicinity. The area was—and is—dominated by Ham House, a stately Jacobean mansion owned today by the National Trust, but for centuries the home of the Dysart Family. Along with its extensive gardens, it is open to the public and hired out for parties and weddings.

Grey Court House is today part of Grey Court School, a secondary comprehensive school opened in 1957 by the Surrey County Council and since the 1960s run by the London Borough of Richmond-upon-Thames. A blue plaque proclaims that "In this house John Henry Newman 1801–1890, later Cardinal Newman, spent some of his early years".

In his essay on "Discipline and Influence" Newman described the house and grounds:

> It is an old-fashioned place, the house may be of the date of George the Second; a square hall

in the middle, and in the centre of it a pillar, and rooms all round. The servants' rooms and offices run off on the right; a rookery covers the left flank, and the drawing-room opens upon the lawn.

There is a large plane tree, with its massive branches, which whilome sustained a swing, when there were children on that lawn, blithely to undergo an exercise of the head, at the very thought of which the grown man sickens. Three formal terraces gradually conduct down to one of the majestic avenues (belonging to the neighbourhood park of a nobleman) the second and third, intersected by grass walks, constitute the kitchen garden. As a boy, I used to stare at the magnificent cauliflowers and large apricots which it furnished for the table, when once one got among the gooseberry bushes in the idle morning.

Because the house is now (2018) part of a school, the gates are sometimes locked, but the house can easily be viewed through them. When the gates are unlocked, it is possible to walk around and up to the front door, and to explore what was once a garden at the back. By contacting the school it is also sometimes possible, with special permission, to arrange for a visit inside, but there is little of interest to see as it is all furnished with modern school equipment and nothing remains of the Newman family or of any other previous owner. The school is, however, very proud of the Newman link: the house is known as Newman House and his memory is much honoured.

A large glass structure has been added to the side—although this is so designed as not to be immediately visible on first sight of the house and does not spoil its general appearance from the front. All is in good repair, although the exterior of the house looks a little shabby, the basement windows covered with dirt and the rooms there clearly not in use, and the other windows in some need of repainting. What were once the gardens are now mostly scrub and the school buildings are immediately adjacent.

There are some other large houses nearby, but Grey Court House is not difficult to find because it is right next to the school which has its own large name-board.

Newman had vivid memories of this childhood home. Describing it all to his friend Henry Wilberforce in 1853 he wrote:

> I have seen our house at Ham once in 1813, in the holidays when my father, brother and myself rode there from Norwood—and the gardener gave us three apricots and my father telling me to choose I took the largest, a thing which still distresses me whenever I think of it.

> And once again in January 23 1836, when I walked there with Bowden and his wife. It was then, I believe, a school—and the fine Trees, which were upon the lawn, were cut down—a large plane, a dozen of tree acacias, with rough barks, as high as the plane—a Spanish chestnut, a larch. A large magnolia, flowering in June I think, went up the house, and the mower's scythe, cutting the lawn, used to

sound so sweetly as I lay in a crib—in a front room at the top.

To find it, you must go down Ham Walk with your back to Lord Dysart's house towards Ham Common. On your right hand, some way down, is a lane called 'Sandy Lane'—our house lay on one side (the further side) of that lane, which formed a boundary, first of the lawn and shrubbery (which tapered almost to a point, between the lane and the paddock) and then of the kitchen garden. Hence some people got over the wall, and stole the grapes. There was no hot house but a small green house in the kitchen garden, which was over a poor billiard room. There I learned to play billiards, having never seen the game played since.

I left the place in September 1807. I recollect the morning we left—and taking leave of it. My mother, my brother Charles, Harriet and I in the carriage—going to Brighton—with my father's horses as far as Ewell (? Is there such a place?) and then posting.

Then a few days later in another letter he wrote:

Our grounds went down to the long Ham walk of double elms. And the house faced a road which led down (I think) to the water—with gentleman's houses on either side. There was a Mr Bradley's on one side, and Lady Parker (I think)—she had a macaw –on the other. Have they covered the whole territory with villas?[4]

The house passed into various hands after the Newman family left. In 1825 it was known as Grove

House and the occupant was William Beebe. In the 1841 census William Beebe was described as a skin— i.e. leather and hides—merchant: he also had premises at Bermondsey skin market. In 1860 the occupant was a Miss Parry and she was still there in 1876. At that time the house continued to be known as Grove House. However, by 1882 it was again known as Grey Court and the occupant was Leslie Fraser D. Duncan who remained there for several years.

In 1897 Colonel John Biddulph lived there: he had served in the Indian Army, and after returning home he became active in Richmond life, sitting on the Urban District Council for many years, and becoming its chairman 1905, and as a Justice of the Peace. He belonged to a distinguished family—one brother became Governor of Gibraltar. Other owners followed, and the final private owner was Bertram Cater who lived there from 1930 to 1940.

Grey Court House was requisitioned by the Army from 1940–42. In the spring of 1943 it became a wartime nursery, opened on March 19th 1943 by Mrs Ernest Brown, wife of the Minister of Health. In 1948 this arrangement was formalised as Grey Court Nursery school, first under Surrey County Council and later the London Borough of Richmond-upon-Thames.[5]

In 1976 the head mistress of the nursery school described it in terms that echo Newman's idyllic childhood memories: Miss Margaret Pegram, head of nursery school for 28 years, said "It had everything a child could ask for, ducks on the duck pond, a river and boats, countryside walks and horses and cows."

She remembered that quite often the teachers had to shoo away cows that wandered too near the school.[6] The nursery proved popular and when its closure was announced in 1975 there were local protests, with three thousand people signing a petition to keep it open, to no avail.[7]

After the nursery's closure the house became part of Grey Court secondary school which stands alongside. The school had opened twenty years earlier with Mr F. W. Nicholson headmaster, the formal ceremony taking place in January 1957 with Lord Hailsham, Minister of Education, and Mr J. C. Thomson, chairman of Surrey County Council Education Committee, among the guests. The school was regarded as a prestige project of the County Council and its opening was a major local event with substantial press coverage. The opening ceremony concluded with a short dedication service finishing with a hymn, "Now thank we all our God", and then the National Anthem.[8]

In the first years of the school's existence little attention seems to have been paid to the Newman family link. But in 1980 a plaque was unveiled on the wall of Grey Court House by local resident Sir Richard Cave—a well-known Catholic who had also arranged for a Catholic parish to be established in Ham. Those attending included Rt Rev. Harold Tripp, auxiliary Bishop of Southwark, Rt Rev. Keith Sutton, Anglican Bishop of Kingston , the Mayor of Richmond Cllr Mrs Norma Millar, and Greater London councillor (later Sir) Edward Leigh.

Grey Court School serves what is now essentially a suburban area although Ham still has very much the feel of a village. There are indeed a good many "villas" now around Grey Court House—some built in the nineteenth century and a great many more in the 20th, with prospect of further building in the 21st. There is a row of shops near Grey Court House, and a pleasant pub just further up Ham Street. There is also—just yards from the house—a small and flourishing Catholic church, dedicated to St Thomas Aquinas, in what was once the village school. This is a thriving parish and is also home to a group of the Ordinariate of Our Lady of Walsingham, of which Blessed John Henry Newman is patron. One memorable summer evening in 2015, the Ordinariate group made a visit to Grey Court House—opened to them specially for this occasion—followed by a picnic supper on the village green, honouring the memory of John Henry Newman in the place he loved.

How to get to Grey Court House

The most interesting—and pleasant—way to reach Grey Court House is on foot along by the Thames. Take the train to Richmond, go down George Street and then turn left to the Old Town Hall and down the steps to the riverside. Your route is up-river in the direction of Kingston.

The walk takes you along by the very attractive riverside public gardens with various restaurants, pubs and cafes, and then, quite suddenly, you are out of the town and at Petersham meadows, where cows are grazing and you are in beautiful countryside. In hot weather, the next stretch can seem quite long, with the river on one side and little shade, but the scenery is glorious and then the woods are reached. There are several paths to the left, each crossing a small stream that runs parallel with the river. Take the path that is marked for Ham House—and as you reach the great mansion, turn to the right and walk along the front of it until Ham Street is reached, and then turn up this road and keep on walking.

Although the river route is attractive, the most logical way to reach Grey Court house is from the main road that runs from Kingston to Richmond. The 65 bus from either town goes along the main road, stopping at the New Inn on Ham Common. Both towns have frequent trains to central London.

EALING, LONDON W5

WHEN NEWMAN WAS seven years old, he was sent to what was then one of the most prestigious schools in England—Great Ealing School. He arrived there on May 1st 1808. The school had a strong academic reputation and was ranked alongside Eton and Harrow by families anxious for their sons to excel.

Ealing today is easily reached from central London by Tube: Ealing Broadway is at the end of the District Line. In the early nineteenth century it would have been perhaps a ride of one and a half to two hours.

The school had extensive grounds which included a cricket green and a swimming pool. Founded in 1698, it stood alongside St Mary's Road near St Mary's Church, and was initially based in the Old Rectory. The school had an "avenue of lime trees that Newman saw felled in full blossom nearly half a century later, and twelve acres of playing fields".[9] Later in the nineteenth century the school it moved a short distance away to where Cairn Avenue now stands. This must have been the time when Newman saw the avenue of lime trees chopped down.

The school closed in 1908 and no trace of it now remains except for a road named Nicholas Gardens. This commemorates the Nicholas family who ran the school.

Newman loved the country area of Ealing and took long walks in the area. In May of 1810 he wrote in his diary "Took a walk to Little Ealing" and a few days later on May 13th "Took a walk to Duke of Kent". This refers to the fact that the Duke of Kent—father of the future Queen Victoria—had a house at Ealing, at Castle Hill.[10]

Among the teachers at the school in Newman's time was the exiled king Louis Phillippe of France. During the nineteenth century famous pupils included William S. Gilbert (of Gilbert and Sullivan fame), scientist Thomas Huxley and author Frederick Marryat.

Newman had to remain at school during one long holiday in 1816, because he was unwell and because the failure of his father's bank brought the crisis that meant that they had to leave their home at Southampton Place. It was during this time that he read a book introducing him to a powerful Evangelical message and he made a definite decision for Christ. The family had always been churchgoers but he now, as he put it "came under the influence of a definite creed"[11], which would shape the whole of his future life and work. He always saw this Evangelical moment as the central Christian experience of his life, on which other events hung. The Newman family's religion had been one of adherence to the Church of England, with Bible reading and prayers, but with no sense that doctrine was really important, and with no concept of a sacramental life: Christianity was a matter of obeying the Ten Commandments and treating Scripture reverently as God's word.

Great Ealing School's atmosphere seems to have been scholarly and friendly, with the boys given a half-holiday every Thursday and regular weekend visits home. Newman became the top pupil, excelling academically.

A visit to Ealing to seek links with Newman is disappointing. St Mary's Church, which Newman would have attended as a boy with the other pupils, is today a magnificent Victorian building, recently restored, evidently home to a thriving parish community and with fine stained glass, glorious sweeping arches and a large gallery. In Newman's day it would have been a small, unremarkable, box-shaped building, of which a print hangs in the present church.

Staff at the church were most welcoming but had no knowledge of there being any link with Newman. A day's exploring, including a cheery pub lunch at the Rose and Crown, and a walk along St Mary's Road and down Cairn Avenue to Nicholas Road, brought no visible sign of any link. A visit to St Mary's church is recommended in that its rebuilding in gothic style reflects the Catholic revival in the Church of England that Newman helped to initiate—and the print of the original church in the entrance area shows how it looked in young Newman's schooldays.

The 65 bus route links this part of Ealing with Ealing Broadway.

VINE COTTAGE, NORWOOD, SOUTH LONDON

I T WAS, AS mentioned, while Newman was at school in Ealing that his father's bank failed and the security they had enjoyed vanished

He was able to pay all his creditors, but the family was impoverished. They left their London home: John remained at school for the summer of 1816 and the rest of the family went to stay a family cottage in what was then the Great North Wood, on the outskirts of Croydon

They had often stayed there before for summer holidays and the children loved it. It was among fields and woods, a place of fresh air and freedom. Their maternal grandmother Elizabeth Newman (1733–1823) and their Aunt Elizabeth "Aunt Betsy" (1765–1852) lived there after leaving their earlier home in Fulham. The area was entirely rural, and the cottage has been described by one author as "a little house set on a remote heath".[12] Norwood was famous for its gypsies and part of the district is still known as Gypsy Hill. The Great North Wood was, as its name implies, vast: its trees supplied wood for, among much else, the great sailing ships of the Royal Navy.

Vine Cottage stood on Knights Hill Green. It seems likely that it was at the bottom of the hill that runs down from where the West Norwood railway station now stands, past St Luke's church (built 1823) and the large public cemetery (again, created later in the nineteenth century). At the top of the hill is The Horns pub, which has existed for centuries and owes its name to the popular local tradition of hunting. At the bottom today (2019) all is busy shops and traffic. A coffee-shop—where the author and researcher for this book settled with maps and talk—might credibly describe itself as being on the site of Vine Cottage.

A booklet on the history of St Luke's church states "The banker father of J.H. Newman kept until 1816 a summer retreat at Vine Cottage on Knights Hill Green below the Horns."[13]

There was a mansion owned by Lord Thurlow at Knights Hill—it was burned down in 1809—and he lived nearby at Knights Hill Farm.

When at Vine Cottage, the Newman family would have worshipped at St Leonard's Church, Streatham. There were at that time no other churches nearby.

The Newmans left Vine Cottage in November 1816, when it was given up as part of the necessary selling of family properties following the closure of John Newman's bank. Young John Henry, writing to his mother from school at Ealing sympathised with his sisters in their plight as they worked to move all their possessions to a new home at Alton in Hampshire: "It must be a laborious work, a labour worthy of Hercules to empty two houses of many years and what with the distance of their destinations from their accustomed home, added to the toil of packing it must be a most arduous undertaking."[14]

How to get to Norwood

A train from London's Victoria station will take you to West Norwood, and the local library (London Borough of Lambeth) will give you what information is available as to the possible whereabouts of the Newman family cottage.

17 GROSVENOR PLACE, LONDON SW1X 7HR

WHEN NEWMAN WENT up to Oxford as a young undergraduate, one of the first friends he made was John Bowden (1798–1844), who was also studying at Trinity College and went on to take honours in mathematics. In 1828 he married Elizabeth, daughter of Sir John Edward Swinburne and they lived at 17 Grosvenor Place, where Newman became a frequent visitor, staying for long periods.

Bowden was not ordained—he went into public service and became Commissioner for Stamps—but was an active member of the Tractarian Movement writing notable essays including *On Gothic Architecture* and *On the Church in the Mediterranean*.

A letter from Bowden to Newman in 1835 gives a flavour of their friendship:

> I cannot tell you how much Elizabeth and I miss you. It is curious, how in these weeks, we established in our minds the impression that your presence with us was the rule and your absence the exception, so that it seems now a strange thing to us that we should be without you.[15]

Bowden died in 1844. Elizabeth and their children later (1846) became Catholics, two sons Charles and John, joining the Birmingham Oratory, and a daughter, Marianne, becoming a nun in the Visitation order.

Elizabeth lived until 1896: in her widowhood she went to live at Fulham where she was active in establishing the Catholic parish.

Newman went to 17 Grosvenor Place—where Elizabeth and the children were still living—in July 1846 shortly after becoming a Catholic and leaving Littlemore. He went to Old Oscott House (Maryvale) in Birmingham first and made a visit to London from there. It seems that Grosvenor Place it was still in a sense his home-from-home. He wrote from there to his old friend Henry Wilberforce to explain in detail his reasons for becoming a Catholic. He also wrote a rather amusing letter to Ambrose St John—who had similarly become a Catholic and would be his closest friend in their ensuing years of being Oratorians together—with an account of the information given to him about living in a Jesuit house in Rome.

The house at 17 Grosvenor Places that Newman knew no longer stands. A much grander building was erected in 1867 and is today the Embassy of the Republic of Ireland. It is listed as being of historic interest, and the Embassy website gives some information about it but there is no mention of any Newman link.

How to get to Grosvenor Place

The nearest tube station is Victoria, which is also a main railway terminus serving Surrey and Sussex. On leaving the station the station, cross Buckingham Palace Road near the statue of Marshal Foch and keep walking. Grosvenor Place is the main road that faces the rear garden wall of Buckingham Palace and Number 17 is clearly marked as the Embassy.

CHURCHES AND SHRINES HONOURING NEWMAN

Brompton Oratory London SW7 2RP

AFTER JOINING THE Catholic Church in 1845 Newman went to Rome where he was ordained a priest and in due course returned to Britain with the plan of establishing the Oratory of St Philip Neri. He did this initially in Birmingham (see separate section) and in due course a London Oratory was also established by a group of Oratorian priests led by Father Frederick William Faber. They began in a converted gin shop in King William Street just off the Strand, and later acquired land in what was then the rural area of Brompton. A large neo-baroque church was built here, the foundation stone laid in 1880 and the church opened by Cardinal Henry Manning in 1884. It has a nave wider than that of St Paul's Cathedral and is today the best-known Catholic church in London after Westminster Cathedral, with a large congregation.

Newman was present at the consecration of the church, and also stayed at the Oratory House while having his portrait painted by Sir John Everett Millais, who lived nearby.

In 1896 a large memorial to Newman was created outside the church, facing on to the Brompton Road. The memorial was designed by Bodley and Garnier.

The statue of Newman is by Leon Joseph Chaullaud (18858–1919) and was commissioned by the 15th Duke of Norfolk, chairman of a committee formed specifically for the purpose of establishing a Newman monument on this site.

The church also has a fine chapel dedicated to Newman, created to mark his beatification by Pope Benedict XVI during his visit to Britain in 2010, and blessed on September 22nd of that year. It carries the words from Newman's funeral plaque: *Ex umbris et imaginibus in veritatem* (out of shadows and imagining into truth).

The district, countryside in the mid-nineteenth century, was steadily built up and by the early twentieth century had become very fashionable. Today it boasts famous shops and smart cafes and restaurants. The great church, officially known as the London Oratory but familiarly known as Brompton Oratory, is a parish church and is also known for fashionable weddings. It has a professional choir and a popular children's choir.

The London Oratory School, founded by the Oratory Fathers at the end of the nineteenth century, is in Seagrave Road, Fulham, and is also famous for its music, with a *schola* that has sung at Europe's and America's great cathedrals.

How to get to Brompton Oratory

Nearest tube: South Kensington. The Oratory is a massive church standing alongside the Victoria and Albert Museum on the Brompton Road.

Church of St Gregory and the Assumption, Warwick Street London W1F 9JR

The first Catholic church that Newman visited was the Church of Our Lady of the Assumption and St Gregory in Warwick Street, London WI. He was a small boy at the time and went with his father: this would have been while they were living at Southampton Place.

Many years later he would write about this in his *Apologia Pro Vita Sua*:

> I had once been into Warwick Street chapel with my father, who, I believe, went to hear a piece of music: all that I bore away from it was the recollection of a pulpit and a preacher and a boy swinging a censer.

The church at Warwick Street is a former Embassy chapel: in the days when the Catholic faith could not be practised openly in Britain, foreign embassies of Catholic countries had their own chapels where Mass was celebrated. This meant that London Catholics could go to Mass there, and many did so. There were English and Irish priests who served these chapels: under the protection of a foreign embassy they could care for the Catholics of London.

From 1724 to 1747 the Portuguese Embassy had a chapel next to the house of its Ambassador, which fronted on to Golden Square. The church's entrance was in Warwick Street, at the back of the Embassy residence. In 1747 the Portuguese left and the Bavarian Embassy took over the house and the chapel. For the next forty years—a time during which pressure on Catholics gradually lessened and, although penal laws still existed, it was in practice easier to attend Mass—the Bavarian Embassy chapel became quite well known.

In 1788 the first major Catholic Relief Act was passed in Parliament: Lord George Gordon, who passionately opposed the Act, made a series of inflammatory anti-Catholic speeches at St George's Fields in Southwark, which provoked what became known as the Gordon riots. Crowds shouting anti-Catholic slogans rampaged through the streets, setting fire to shops and homes and chapels—any building that was thought to be "Popish". Many people were killed and the riots were only finally quelled by military intervention.

The Bavarian Embassy chapel was one of the Catholic buildings destroyed. The Bavarian ambassador, whose home was also damaged, had to move elsewhere and allowed the site to be acquired by the Bishop of the London District, Bishop Talbot, who raised funds to build a new church. This was opened on the feast of St Gregory in 1789.

The church is in the diocese of Westminster and has played a major role in the diocese over the years. Today it is, fittingly, in the care of the Ordinariate of Our Lady of Walsingham, of which John Henry Newman is the patron. There is a portrait of Newman in the Lady Chapel, to the right of the main sanctuary. It was placed there in 2016 during the Ordinariate's Chrism Mass in Holy Week, by Archbishop Mennini, then Apostolic Nuncio to the United Kingdom.

The picture is a copy of one in Trinity College, Oxford, where Newman studied as an undergraduate.

The Rectory for the Warwick Street church is at 24, Golden Square, adjoining the rear of the church, and is the residence of the Ordinary of the Ordinariate of Our Lady of Walsingham, currently Rt Rev. Keith Newton.

How to get to the Church of Our Lady of the Assumption and St Gregory, Warwick Street

Nearest tube: Piccadilly Circus. Take the northern exit—away from Regent Street—and walk up the pedestrianised shopping area towards the St James pub and then into Warwick Street.

Tyburn Convent Chapel, near Marble Arch London W2 2LJ

Tyburn was for centuries the grisly site of execution in London. From 1196 until 1783, criminals were killed here: sometimes by hanging, sometimes by the even more cruel death of hanging, drawing and quartering. The *Ty* burn or river flowed here across open land—the criminals were brought out from Newgate prison, sometimes on a cart, sometimes dragged on a hurdle, and crowds gathered to watch as the sentence was carried out.

To Catholics, this is now a sacred place, because from 1535 to 1681 over 100 Catholic men were martyred here—not because of any wrongdoing but simply because they were Catholic priests, in the years when Catholicism was outlawed. Among those who met their deaths with courage here were St Edmund Campion and St Ralph Sherwin. Both had been cruelly tortured in the Tower of London, fingernails torn out, bodies stretched on the rack.

Campion and Sherwin were among the 40 martyrs canonised by Pope Paul VI in 1970. By that time a convent had been established near the site of execution, as a place of perpetual adoration of Christ in the Blessed Sacrament, and a place of prayer and pilgrimage. Today it attracts pilgrims from all over the world, and the Benedictine sisters who run the shrine have become something of a national institution as the "Tyburn nuns".

In 1991 a plaque was unveiled in the convent chapel to mark a special link with John Henry Newman. The convent is at number 5/7, Hyde Park Place, and in the nineteenth century this was the home of Mrs George Hope, sister-in-law of James Robert Hope-Scott, a great friend of Newman. Hope-Scott, a lawyer, was an early supporter of the Tractarian movement, became a Catholic in 1851, and remained in contact with Newman throughout the rest of his life. When Hope-Scott died, Newman preached at his funeral in the Jesuit church at Farm Street, and afterwards went on to 7 Hyde Park Place to lunch with Mrs George Hope. This visit is commemorated in the plaque, which is on the rear wall of the Adoration Chapel. It carries an engraving of Newman and one of Hope-Scott and was unveiled by Archbishop Luigi Barbarito, the Apostolic Nuncio to Great Britain, on June 11th 1991, in the presence of members of the Scott family.

How to get to Tyburn Convent

Nearest tube: Marble Arch. Turn right on leaving the tube station, and cross the big junction at the corner of Edgeware Road and walk down the Bayswater Road, with Hyde Park on your left. The convent and its chapel at 8 Hyde Park Place are easy to see: a large Cross hangs on the wall and a stone commemorates the deaths of Catholic martyrs. The chapel is open to all throughout the day.

Church of the Most Precious Blood, London SE1 1TN: London's newest Newman shrine

The church of the Most Precious Blood at The Borough, London Bridge was built in the 1880s. In 2012 the church and the parish were given into the care of the Ordinariate of Our Lady of Walsingham, and a shrine to John Henry Newman was established to the left of the main sanctuary, matching a shrine to Our Lady standing on the right-hand side.

The Newman shrine was blessed by Archbishop Peter Smith of Southwark on Trinity Sunday 2013 at a Mass concelebrated with the parish priest Rev Christopher Pearson of the Ordinariate. The establishment of the shrine followed a week of Newman celebrations including a lecture and a display about Newman's life and work.

In April 1848, following his return from Rome where he had been ordained a Catholic priest, Newman was asked by Cardinal Nicholas Wiseman to preach some evening sermons at St George's in

Southwark. Later that year (4ᵗʰ July 1848) the new Pugin church of St George was opened and in 1850 it became the cathedral for the newly created diocese of Southwark. It is not clear if Newman's sermons were at the old St George's chapel in St George's Fields, or the new church. Later a story developed that Newman had said his first Mass as a Catholic in St George's but this is not the case.

Precious Blood Church was established some years later as a mission church from St George's.

How to get to the Church of the Most Precious Blood, Borough

Nearest tube: London Bridge or Borough. The church is in O'Meara Street, which runs between Union Street and Southwark Street, off the Borough High Street. You can also walk to the church from the City by crossing London Bridge to reach the Borough High Street. The Church of the Most Precious Blood is in fact the nearest Catholic church to Newman's birthplace.

OTHER PLACES IN LONDON WITH NEWMAN LONDON CONNECTIONS

FTER NEWMAN'S FATHER'S death in 1824, Mrs Newman and her daughters went to live for a time with Aunt Betsy at 69, The Moorings, **Strand-on-the-Green, Chiswick,** and Newman himself often stayed with them there.[16] Aunt Betsy earlier lived at Fulham, and Newman in later life recalled family visits there. The house apparently later became a chemist's shop. Its exact location is not now known.

There is a **portrait of Newman** (by Emmeline Deane, 1888) and a **bust** (by Thomas Woolner 1866) of Newman in the **National Portrait Gallery**, London WC2H 0HE. Nearest tube: Charing Cross. Newman also had his portrait painted by Sir John Everett Millais (1829–1896), and **Millais House**, his home and studio—where Newman went every day to sit for the painting, staying at Brompton Oratory for this purpose—is at 7, Cromwell Place, South Kensington SW7 2JN: it has a blue plaque commemorating Millais. Nearest tube: South Kensington.

Westminster Cathedral has a mosaic of Newman, up on the left-hand wall as you walk up the main aisle. It depicts him with his eyes closed, presumably in prayer. The mosaic is by Tom Philips and was blessed after the 5.30pm Mass on 21ˢᵗ September 2008. The Cathedral was opened in 1903 and consecrated in 1910: Pope St John Paul and Pope Benedict XVI celebrated Mass there on their respective visits in 1982 and 2010. The first public performance of Elgar's setting of Newman's *Dream of Gerontius* was in the Cathedral in 1903. Nearest tube: Victoria.

The Catholic Chaplaincy for the **University of London** is named **Newman House** and is at 111 Grower Street, London WC1E 6AR. Nearest tube: Euston

St Mary's University at Twickenham has a bust of John Henry Newman in its Senior Common Room, and Bishop Philip Egan lectured here on Newman's *Idea of a University* in 2018. Nearest railway station: Strawberry Hill.

PLACES OUTSIDE OF LONDON ASSOCIATED WITH JOHN HENRY NEWMAN

THE TWO MOST important places in Newman's long life were **Oxford**—where he was a scholar, Fellow of Oriel College, vicar of the University Church, and effective founder of the Oxford Movement which changed the face of the Church of England—and **Birmingham**, where he lived first at Old Oscott House (now Maryvale) and later established the Birmingham Oratory.

Alton, Hampshire

But Newman also lived briefly with his parents at Alton in Hampshire where his father, following the closure of his bank, attempted to start a brewing firm. This failed in 1821 he was declared bankrupt, dying three years later. By this time Newman was at Oxford. He became head of the family and took responsibility for providing for his mother and sisters.

A plaque at number 59, High Street, Alton reads "John Henry Newman, later cardinal, lived here with his parents 1816–1819." The house was built around 1769 and owned by the Baverstock family.

The local Catholic parish, St Mary's, is proud of this link. St Mary's, in Normandy Street, is a modern building, opened in 1965. Its website reads:

> A wonderful fact about our parish is that Blessed John Henry Newman's family lived here for three years, when his father became manager of the local brewery. His home on the high street is now an estate agent but there is a Blue Plaque to commemorate his memory.

The local Catholic deanery is named in honour of Newman.

Oxford

John Henry Newman went up to Oxford in 1817 when he was still in his middle teens. Accounts of his departure from the family home for the preliminary interview for university suggest that his father was, up to the last minute, uncertain whether to send the boy to Oxford or to Cambridge. With the carriage waiting, Oxford was chosen, and in due course the teenager became an undergraduate at **Trinity College**. He formally entered the College as a Commoner in December 1816, and took up residence there the following June. He had been a brilliant student at school and quickly established himself as such at Trinity too. He was elected a scholar in 1818. He also made a circle of friends, notable among them John Bowden (see the story at 17 Grosvenor Place, above). He and Bowden published a poem together, "St Bartholomew's Eve", which brought them both to prominence.

While at Trinity, Newman received Holy Communion in the Anglican church for the first time. His previous Sunday religious devotions had centred on Mattins and Evensong: it was unusual at that time for Communion to be celebrated with any frequency in Anglican churches, and this would be one of the major issues addressed by the Oxford Movement.

Newman seems to have overworked during his final year at Trinity, and failed to gain a good degree, barely scraping a pass. But, on the strength of his known work and abilities, he was later awarded a Fellowship at **Oriel College.** Here he spent important years. He had already decided to seek ordination in the Church of England—abandoning some brief earlier thoughts about becoming a lawyer—and on 13th June 1824 he was ordained deacon at **Christ Church**, Oxford, and priest on 29th May 1825, also at Christ Church. He began his pastoral ministry in the parish of **St Clement's, Oxford**, and was also briefly vice-president of St Alban's Hall. In 1826 he resigned both to become a tutor at Oriel. In February 1828 he became vicar of **St Mary's University Church**.

He also had care of the parish at **Littlemore**, a poor village on the outskirts of the city. Here he built a church, created a school for the children, and worked among the impoverished people, notably during a grim cholera epidemic. The foundation stone of the church was laid by his mother, and both she and Newman's sisters assisted him in parish work.

The *Tracts for the Times*, which launched the Oxford Movement, were published throughout the 1830s and by the end of the decade Newman was a major national figure and the Church of England was experiencing a self-questioning and sense of a call to renewal of purpose and direction with long-lasting results. Newman was on his own journey, resigning as a fellow of Oriel and as vicar of St Mary's in 1843, preaching his last sermon at Littlemore on "The parting of friends". He went to live in retirement in a small set of rooms he had created out of some cottages at Littlemore. It was here that he was received into the Catholic Church by Father—now Blessed—Dominic Barberi in 1845.

All of the places mentioned here are worth visiting and have mementoes of Newman, especially **Oriel College** where the chapel depicts him in a stained glass window and a small shrine has been created in his old rooms, and **Littlemore** where a full Newman Centre has been established with his Library and private chapel preserved in their original state.

Oriel College

Founded in 1326, the College is dedicated to the Blessed Virgin Mary. Oriel is immensely proud of its association with Newman, and his room there, which adjoins the chapel, has been preserved as an Oratory.

Newman served as chaplain of Oriel from 1826 to 1833. The rooms that he occupied are in fact over the chapel entrance. Part of one room was used for a time as a larder, but when Newman took over the rooms it seems that he used this area for private prayer. In 1991 it was decided to turn this into an oratory in his memory. There a fine stained glass window depicting him was created by Douglas Hogg to a design by Vivienne Craig. It was put in place in 2001. Newman is shown along with the College's fourteenth-century founders and surrounded by angels. St Mary's University Church, and Littlemore, complete the scene along with extracts from his writings.

It is possible for groups to visit the Chapel and the Newman Oratory but it is necessary to make a special appointment. The easiest thing to do is to write: Oriel College, Oxford OX1 4EW or email: lodge@oriel.ox.ac.uk

Trinity College

There is a bust of Newman at Trinity College, where he began his Oxford life. It stands by the Garden Quad and depicts him as a Cardinal. Trinity, founded in 1555, is in Broad Street: it has a fine chapel and extensive gardens and it is possible to visit at certain times. There is information on the College website www.trinity.ox.ac.uk

The University Church

In 1828 Newman was appointed vicar of St Mary's, the University Church. Here he preached the famous sermons which made him known across the University. Undramatic, spoken in a gentle voice but with great sincerity, the sermons touched the hearts of the undergraduates and word of them spread: the young men attended in vast numbers. The sermons played a major role in the Oxford Movement, causing an immense stir in the Church of England and introducing a revival in its whole sense of mission and identity.

The church stands on the north side of the High Street and welcomes visitors. Services are open to anyone, and guided tours are also available.

Littlemore

Newman ministered for several years at Littlemore, a poor district in the care of the University Church, some distance from the city itself. It had no church, and Newman raised money and built one, the foundation stone being laid by his mother. The church was dedicated in 1836 and Newman, writing to a friend, described it all: "We had a profusion of bright flowers, in bunches, all about the chapel. The Bishop was much pleased. There were a number of details which made it a most delightful day, and long, I hope, may it be remembered here."[17]

Newman worked hard among the poor in Littlemore, visiting the sick, establishing classes in which the children learned some basic skills, running regular catechism lessons, and forming a popular choir which he led himself on his violin. The catechism classes became known in Oxford, and undergraduates started to attend. In 1843, seeking solitude for study and reflection, Newman bought a small set of shabby buildings on the edge of the village, had them refurbished so that they offered some simple accommodation, and formed "The College". He resigned as vicar, preaching a final sermon on "The Parting of Friends" and retired to this College. It was here, two years later, that he was received into the Catholic Church by Blessed Dominic Barberi.

"I am this night expecting Father Dominic, the Passionist, in his way from Aston in Staffordshire to Belgium ... and he, please God, will admit me tomorrow or Friday into what I believe to be the one true Fold of Christ", Newman wrote to Mrs Bowden, widow of his old friend, on October 8th 1845.[18] The buildings at Littlemore, donated by Newman to an Anglican clergyman friend, were later used as almshouses and in the 1950s were acquired by the Birmingham Oratory: today The College is a research and study centre run by the sisters of The Work, an international religious order. They welcome pilgrims to visit the library, to pray in Newman's chapel, to make use of the extensive research material on Newman, to enjoy the peace of the small garden, or to attend one of the regular events, lectures, etc held through the year. It is also possible to arrange to stay for some days, for a retreat or simply for a quiet time and can be reached at: thework@uk2.net or by post: Ambrose Cottage, 9 College Lane Littlemore Oxon OX4 4LQ.

Newman loved Littlemore. His departure following his reception into the Catholic Church, remained in his memory for the rest of his life.[19]

The church of St Mary and St Nicholas, built by Newman during his time as vicar, and containing a monument to his mother, is open to visitors and has regular services. There is also a modern Catholic church dedicated to Bl. Dominic Barberi, the centre of a flourishing parish.

The Oratory Church of St Aloysius

Newman had hoped to establish an Oratory in Oxford, but it did not happen in his lifetime. One hundred years after his death, however, the Oratorians were given charge of the Catholic parish church of St Aloysius. This is today a flourishing Oratory parish and is worth a visit. Every year, the Oratorians organise an evening Walk from the church to Littlemore, on October 8th, stopping at all the places along the way that have a link with Newman, and finishing with prayers in Littlemore's church of Bl. Dominic Barberi and with refreshments at The College.

The Oxford Oratory Church of St Aloysius is on Woodstock Road and its website is www.oxfordoratory.org.uk

Birmingham

Newman, opening the Catholic chapter in his life in the Autumn of 1845, was offered a refuge at Old Oscott House, in what was then a rural area on the outskirts of Birmingham.

The house had been owned by the Bromwich family, who were Catholic recusants, and was for many years a Mass centre used for local Catholic families. Towards the end of the 18th the anti-Catholic laws were eased by various Catholic Relief Acts in Parliament, and Andrew Bromwich gave the house to the Church so that it could be used for the Catholic community emerging from the shadows. From 1794 until 1838 Old Oscott House was a seminary—the first to be established in England since the Reformation. Now, in the 1840s, with the seminary established in new purpose-built premises nearby, it became Newman's new home: he went there with the small community of friends who had gathered around him at Littlemore and were now Catholic.

Newman's room adjoined the chapel and this gave him great consolation. The community established there would in due course form the basis of the Oratory, in the footsteps of St Philip Neri, that he would form in Birmingham. There was a daily routine of prayer and study. Initially they had no priest so they walked across the fields to Birmingham for Mass. In due course Newman went to Rome where he was ordained, and on return he formally established an Oratory, and give the house the name of Maryvale.

As the community grew and flourished, Newman acquired a site in Birmingham where the Oratory could begin full-scale parish work, and where a fine church and house where built. Maryvale became briefly a centre for another religious community, the Oblates of Mary Immaculate, and then an orphanage run by the Sisters of Mercy. This flourished for over 130 years serving the needs of large numbers of children. An extra wing was built to accommodate the children and a sports field laid out for them. The orphanage closed in 1980 and Archbishop George Dwyer established a catechetical training centre which later became the Maryvale Institute, opened by his successor Archbishop Maurice Couve de Murville.

The Maryvale Institute is an international Catholic study centre offering graduate and post-graduate studies in theology and Church history, together with

courses in parish catechetics and family ministry.
Newman's memory is venerated and his daily timetable is among other memorabilia on display in the hall.
Mass is celebrated daily in the chapel, and a community of Brigettine sisters cares for the students and
lecturers through the year. Extra rooms, including a
library and lecture halls, together with accommodation for the Brigettine community and visiting staff,
have been added to the house, in sympathetic style.

Maryvale is no longer in the countryside but is
approached down a curving drive from a busy main
road. A Catholic primary school, secondary school and
parish church stand nearby, together with a convent
which is home to the Sisters of the Blessed Virgin
Mary. These are nuns who were formerly part of the
Anglican community of St Mary the Virgin, Wantage.
When the Ordinariate of Our Lady of Walsingham was
established by Pope Benedict XVI, they joined it and
came into full communion with the Catholic Church,
and after first receiving hospitality from the Benedictine nuns at St Cecilia's Abbey at Ryde on the Isle of
Wight, they were in due course given a convent of their
own here next door to Maryvale.

It is possible to visit Maryvale—there are regular
buses from central Birmingham and taxis from New
Street station—and there are various events throughout the year to which the public are invited. The house
has a wide lawn in front, with a statue of Our Lady. A
long porch runs along the front of the house and
extends towards the chapel which has its own
entrance to one side. Students who come for weekend
residential courses can have the option of using

Newman's old room. The house's age and style give Maryvale its own special feel—one student described its "sloping staircases and unexpected bathrooms"—and it lends itself comfortably to long talkative evenings in the students' common room, or sunny afternoons out on the lawn.

Maryvale also has a shrine to the Sacred Heart—established in recusant times and still honoured. There is an annual outdoor Mass and procession around the grounds, keeping up a tradition that now stretches across centuries.

For more information see: www.maryvale.ac.uk

St Mary's College, Oscott

Better known as "Oscott Seminary", this is some two miles from Maryvale. Here men are trained for the priesthood. Pope Benedict XVI visited here in 2010 to meet seminarians from across Britain. The seminary began at Maryvale in the 18th century and moved to its present site in 1838. The fine nineteenth century buildings include a magnificent chapel by Augustus Welby Pugin. It was here that Newman preached his famous "Second Spring" sermon to the assembled Catholic Bishops of England and Wales in July 1852. The College has an important library and collection of Catholic recusant materials. It is a working seminary and so not usually open to the public, but information on visits is available from the website: oscott.net or by email: enquiries@oscott.org

Birmingham Oratory

Newman established the Oratory at Maryvale in 1848 and later moved it to Birmingham, beginning in an old gin distillery before finally settling the Oratory on its present site in Edgbaston in 1852. Here Newman spent fruitful years. Here he wrote his famous *Apologia Pro Vita Sua* explaining his life's spiritual journey. Here he established a school, which would later move to Woodcote in Oxfordshire where it still flourishes. Here he learned, in the pontificate of Leo XIII, that he had been appointed a Cardinal. By the time he died in 1890, he had become a national figure.

After Newman's day, it was felt that a larger building was needed, and so the present church was begun in 1902 and formally opened in 1909. It is the main national shrine to Newman, and in the Oratory House his room is preserved along with his books and other memorabilia. Pope Benedict XVI visited here in 2010 when he came to Britain to beatify Newman. He unveiled a plaque on the outside wall.

Pope Benedict's 2010 State visit to Britain was a highlight of his pontificate. The beatification Mass took place at Cofton Park, attended by thousands: it included Newman's hymn "Firmly I believe and Truly". It was 130 years since Newman's death. Britain had contributed a new feast-day for the Church's calendar: it was announced that Newman's feast-day would be October 9th, the day in which he was received into the full communion of the Catholic Church.

The Birmingham Oratory welcomes visitors and it is possible to visit Newman's room. The website is at www.birminghamoratory.org.uk

FINALLY ...

I N 2010 POPE BENEDICT XVI, as the climax of a
State Visit to Britain, at a Mass attended by thousands, formally declared John Henry Newman to
be Blessed. It seems fitting to end this book with the
words that were spoken by the Vicar of Christ, at the
Mass at Cofton Park near Birmingham on that occasion.

Dear Brothers and Sisters in Christ,

This day that has brought us together here in
Birmingham is a most auspicious one. In the
first place, it is the Lord's day, Sunday, the day
when our Lord Jesus Christ rose from the dead
and changed the course of human history for
ever, offering new life and hope to all who live
in darkness and in the shadow of death. That
is why Christians all over the world come
together on this day to give praise and thanks
to God for the great marvels he has worked for
us. This particular Sunday also marks a significant moment in the life of the British nation,
as it is the day chosen to commemorate the
seventieth anniversary of the Battle of Britain.
For me as one who lived and suffered through
the dark days of the Nazi regime in Germany,
it is deeply moving to be here with you on this
occasion, and to recall how many of your
fellow citizens sacrificed their lives, coura-
geously resisting the forces of that evil ideology. My thoughts go in particular to nearby
Coventry, which suffered such heavy bom-

bardment and massive loss of life in November 1940. Seventy years later, we recall with shame and horror the dreadful toll of death and destruction that war brings in its wake, and we renew our resolve to work for peace and reconciliation wherever the threat of conflict looms. Yet there is another, more joyful reason why this is an auspicious day for Great Britain, for the Midlands, for Birmingham. It is the day that sees Cardinal John Henry Newman formally raised to the altars and declared Blessed.

I thank Archbishop Bernard Longley for his gracious welcome at the start of Mass this morning. I pay tribute to all who have worked so hard over many years to promote the cause of Cardinal Newman, including the Fathers of the Birmingham Oratory and the members of the Spiritual Family *Das Werk*. And I greet everyone here from Great Britain, Ireland, and further afield; I thank you for your presence at this celebration, in which we give glory and praise to God for the heroic virtue of a saintly Englishman.

England has a long tradition of martyr saints, whose courageous witness has sustained and inspired the Catholic community here for centuries. Yet it is right and fitting that we should recognize today the holiness of a confessor, a son of this nation who, while not called to shed his blood for the Lord, nevertheless bore eloquent witness to him in the course of a long life devoted to the priestly ministry, and especially to preaching, teaching, and writing. He is worthy to take his place in a long line of saints and scholars from these islands, Saint Bede, Saint Hilda, Saint Aelred, Blessed Duns Scotus, to name but a few. In Blessed John Henry, that tradition of gentle scholarship, deep human wisdom and profound love for the Lord has borne rich fruit, as a sign of the abiding presence of the Holy Spirit deep within the heart of God's people, bringing forth abundant gifts of holiness.

Cardinal Newman's motto, *Cor ad cor loquitur*, or "Heart speaks unto heart", gives us an insight into his understanding of the Christian life as a call to holiness, experienced as the profound desire of the human heart to enter into intimate communion with the Heart of God. He reminds us that faithfulness to prayer gradually transforms us into the divine likeness. As he wrote in one of his many fine sermons, "a habit of prayer, the practice of turning to God and the unseen world in every season, in every place, in every emergency—prayer, I say, has what may be called a natural effect in spiritualizing and elevating the soul. A man is no longer what he was before; gradually ... he has imbibed a new set of ideas, and become imbued with fresh principles" (*Parochial and Plain Sermons*, iv, 230–231). Today's Gospel tells us that no one can be the servant of two masters (cf. Lk 16:13), and Blessed John Henry's teaching on prayer explains how the faithful Christian is definitively taken into the service of the one true Master, who alone has a claim to our unconditional devotion (cf. Mt 23:10). Newman helps us to understand what this means for our daily lives: he tells us that our divine Master has assigned a specific task to each one of us, a "definite service", committed uniquely to every single person: "I have my mission", he wrote, "I am a link in a chain, a bond of connexion between persons. He has not created me for naught. I shall do good, I shall do his work; I shall be an angel of peace, a preacher of truth in my own place ... if I do but keep his commandments and serve him in my calling" (*Meditations and Devotions*, 301–2).

The definite service to which Blessed John Henry was called involved applying his keen intellect and his prolific pen to many of the most pressing "subjects of the day". His insights into the relationship between faith and reason, into the vital place of revealed religion in civilized society, and into the need for a broadly-based and wide-ranging approach to education were not only of profound importance for Victorian England, but continue today to inspire and enlighten many all over the world. I would like to pay particular tribute to his vision for education, which has done so much to shape the ethos that is the driving force behind Catholic schools and colleges today. Firmly opposed to any reductive or utilitarian approach, he sought to achieve an educational environment in which intellectual training, moral discipline and religious commitment would come together. The project to found a Catholic University in Ireland provided him with an opportunity to develop his ideas on the subject, and the collection of discourses that he published as The Idea of a University holds up an ideal from which all those engaged in academic formation can continue to learn. And indeed, what better goal could teachers of religion set themselves than Blessed John Henry's famous appeal for an intelligent, well-instructed laity: "I want a laity, not arrogant, not rash in speech, not disputatious, but men who know their religion, who enter into it, who know just where they stand, who know what they hold and what they do not, who know their creed so well that they can give an account of it, who know so much of history that they can defend it" (*The Present Position of Catholics in England*, ix, 390). On this day when the author of those words is raised to the altars, I pray that, through his intercession and example, all who are engaged in the task of teaching and catechesis will be inspired to greater effort by the vision he so clearly sets before us.

While it is John Henry Newman's intellectual legacy that has understandably received most attention in the vast literature devoted to his life and work, I prefer on this occasion to conclude with a brief reflection on his life as a priest, a pastor of souls. The warmth and humanity underlying his appreciation of the pastoral ministry is beautifully expressed in another of his famous sermons: "Had Angels been your priests, my brethren, they could not have condoled with you, sympathized with you, have had compassion on you, felt tenderly for you, and made allowances for you, as we can; they could not have been your patterns and guides, and have led you on from your old selves into a new life, as they can who come from the midst of you" ("Men, not Angels: the Priests of the Gospel", *Discourses to Mixed Congregations*, 3). He lived out that profoundly human vision of priestly ministry in his devoted care for the people of Birmingham during the years that he spent at the Oratory he founded, visiting the sick and the poor, comforting the bereaved, caring for those in prison. No wonder that on his death so many thousands of people lined the local streets as his body was taken to its place of burial not half a mile from here. One hundred and twenty years later, great crowds have assembled once again to rejoice in the Church's solemn recognition of the outstanding holiness of this much-loved father of souls. What better way to express the joy of this moment than by turning to our heavenly Father in heartfelt thanksgiving, praying in the words that Blessed John Henry Newman placed on the lips of the choirs of angels in heaven:

Praise to the Holiest in the height
And in the depth be praise;
In all his words most wonderful,
Most sure in all his ways!
(*The Dream of Gerontius*).

BIBLIOGRAPHY

Apologia Pro Vita Sua John Henry Newman 1863. London, Sheed and Ward 1945, new edition with introduction by Meriol Trevor 1979.

The Letters and Diaries of John Henry Newman. Oxford: Oxford University Press 1988.

Newman at Littlemore Bernard Bassett SJ, Leominster: Gracewing 2019.

Pilgrim Journey: John Henry Newman 1801–1845. Vincent Ferrer Blehl SJ London, Burns and Oates 2001.

John Henry Newman: a biography. Ian Ker. Oxford: Oxford University Press 1988.

Newman and his Age. Sheridan Gilley. London: Darton Longman and Todd 1988.

John Henry Newman. James Arthur and Guy Nicholls. London: Continuum 2007.

Ever Yours Affly: John Henry Newman and his female circle. Joyce Sugg. Leominster: Gracewing 1996.

Snapdragon on the Wall: The story of John Henry Newman. Joyce Sugg. Leominster: Gracewing 2001.

Newman William Barry London: Hodder and Stoughton 1945.

Catalogue: *Cardinal Newman 1801–90 A centenary exhibition.* Susan Foister, National Portrait Gallery 1990.

Blessed John Henry Newman: A Richly Illustrated Portrait. ed Kathleen Dietz and Mary-Birgit Dechant Leominster: Gracewing 2010.

Praise to the Holiest in the Height

Praise to the Holiest in the height,
and in the depth be praise;
in all his words most wonderful,
most sure in all his ways!

O loving wisdom of our God!
When all was sin and shame,
a second Adam to the fight
and to the rescue came.

O wisest love! that flesh and blood,
which did in Adam fail,
should strive afresh against the foe,
should strive, and should prevail;

and that the highest gift of grace
should flesh and blood refine:
God's presence and his very self,
and essence all-divine.

O generous love! that he who smote
in man for man the foe,
the double agony in Man
for man should undergo.

And in the garden secretly,
and on the cross on high,
should teach his brethren, and inspire
to suffer and to die.

Praise to the Holiest in the height,
and in the depth be praise;
in all his words most wonderful,
most sure in all his ways!

JOHN HENRY NEWMAN

ENDNOTES

1   See https://en.wikipedia.org/wiki/St_Benet_Fink.

2   See web link www.ucl.ac.uk/bloomsbury-project/streets/southampton_street.htm.

3   See http://studyabroad.arcadia.edu/find-a-program/our-centers/london/.

4   Letter to Wilberforce in W. Ward, *Life of Newman* (Longman, Green and Co 1912), vol 2, p. 22.

5   Unsigned notes in the local history archive, London Borough of Richmond, in Richmond Old Town Hall.

6   Richmond Herald newspaper 22.7.1976.

7   Richmond and Twickenham Times newspaper Jan 24 1975 "3,000 sign plea to halt nursery school shut-down".

8   London Borough of Richmond local archives, Old Town Hall: programme and Order of Service.

9   Sheridan Gilley, *Newman and his Age*, p. 10.

10 *The Letters and Diaries of John Henry Newman*, p. 6.

11 J. H. Newman, *Apologia Pro Vita Sua*, p. 2.

12 J. Sugg, *Ever Yours affly*, Gracewing 1996.

13 *St Luke West Norwood*, Holdaway and Lambert 1974, copy held at West Norwood library, London Borough of Lambeth.

14 Letter 30 Oct 1816, *The Letters and Diaries of John Henry Newman*, p. 26.

15 See web link www.newmanreader.org/biography/mozley/volume2/file4.html.

16 See www.chiswickw4.com.

17 Quoted in Bassett, B. Newman at Littlemore, p. 20.

[18]   Quoted in Bassett, B. Newman at Littlemore, p. 47.

[19]   "Last days at Littlemore" in W. Ward, *Life of Cardinal Newman* (Longman, Green and Co 1912) Vol 1, p. 116.

Lightning Source UK Ltd.
Milton Keynes UK
UKHW011238091119
353155UK00001B/2/P